Niagara-on-the-Lake

ST. MARK'S CHURCH, NIAGARA.

NIAGARA-ON-THE-LAKE

The Old Historical Town

by
Nick and Helma Mika
with
Nancy Butler and Joy Ormsby

Mika Publishing Company
Belleville, Ontario
1990

Acknowledgements

Some of our books have been written on the advice of our good friends, and this one is not an exception. When we decided to take a holiday, we chose Niagara-on-the-Lake and enjoyed our visit more each day.

The highlights of our stay were attending the famous Shaw Festival and visiting the Old Book Store on Queen Street. The charming proprietor of this unique store, Laura McFadden, gave us a brief and fascinating story about the old historical town and suggested we publish a new book about this community.

After taking numerous pictures of the historical buildings, visiting Fort George, Fort Mississauga, Navy Hall, Butler's Barracks and the Historical Society Museum on Castlereagh Street and meeting curator Bill Severin, we decided to go ahead with the book.

Our first priority was to contact the president of the Historical Society Nancy Butler and local historian Joy Ormsby, who both agreed to write articles on the activities of the Historical Society and provided us with introductions and descriptions of the various historical buildings. They contributed some excellent material concerning these important subjects. We sincerely thank them for their valuable time. We would also like to express our appreciation to Judie Dyck, General Manager of the Niagara-on-the-Lake Chamber of Commerce, for supplying material concerning the historical and commercial aspects of the town, and to The Niagara Advance for back issues of their newspaper.

Niagara-on-the Lake, The Old Historical Town
Copyright © Mika Publishing Company, 1990
ISBN 0-921341-36-9
Printed and bound in Canada

Historical Background

At the mouth of the Niagara River, overlooking Lake Ontario and the American Fort of Niagara, stands the picturesque town of Niagara-on-the-Lake. The streets, shadowed by maple and oak trees, are the setting for charming houses on grounds graced with a variety of flowers blossoming from early spring until late fall. Some of the houses and shops are decorated with Canadian flags signifying their owners' love of country and belief in the ideals of their forefathers.

The community was settled at the close of the American Revolution by Butler's Rangers and Loyalist refugees arriving from New York State, Connecticut and Pennsylvania. It was Governor Haldimand who in September 1779 suggested to John Butler to cultivate land and prepare for settlement on the west bank of the Niagara River to accommodate "His Majesty's loyal subjects who had been driven from their homes". The following summer some land was cleared and log barracks were built at the corner of what is now Wellington and Ricardo streets. The small community consisting at first of five families living in fairly comfortable dwellings were joined in 1781 by a group of associated Loyalists and discharged soldiers from various regiments. The place was renamed West Niagara, to distinguish it from Fort Niagara, having first been known as Butlersburg after Loyalist leader John Butler.

As time went by, the population of the settlement was again boosted by enterprising pioneers arriving from England, Scotland, Ireland, France, Germany and Russia. The Loyalists along with the newcomers created businesses and built houses reflecting the spirit and influence of American architecture as well as the originality and fashion of the Old World. The old section of the town still displays these influences of Georgian-Loyalist, Regency, Classic Revival, Gothic Revival, Italianate and Victorian style of architecture.

As well as being noted for its many beautiful homes, Niagara-on-the-Lake is steeped in history, a place with more firsts to its credit than any other community of its size in the province. Some twenty historical plaques erected in various places testify to this, as they commemorate important events in the town's past.

It was here at Niagara that in 1792 the first census in Upper Canada was taken. That year, Upper Canada's first parliament assembled here for its first of five sessions, and the province's first grist-mill began grinding flour for the settlers. Soon after a Masonic Lodge, the first in Upper Canada, was opened at Niagara and the first Agricultural Society was formed by its inhabitants. A printing press brought to the settlement produced the province's first newspaper, "The Upper Canada Gazette". What is considered to be the first brick building in Upper Canada, was erected at Niagara as early as 1795 and in 1800 the first library was established here.

When Quebec had been divided into the Upper

and Lower Canada, the pioneer settlement at Niagara was proclaimed the first capital of Upper Canada by Lieutenant-Governor John Graves Simcoe who changed the name of the place from West Niagara to Newark. When Simcoe departed Upper Canada, the name was restored to Niagara and remained so until 1906 when the community adopted perhaps the prettiest name of them all, Niagara-on-the-Lake.

The Seven Years' War, the conquest of Quebec and the American Revolution which brought Butler's Rangers and Loyalists to the Niagara Peninsula, all played their parts in shaping the landscape of the region. In the charming little town of Niagara-on-the-Lake much of the rich heritage of Ontario has been preserved in restored old homes and shops, museums and historic sites.

Development of the Old Town of Niagara

In November 1791, Augustus Jones, assisted by chain bearers and axemen hired at a rate "not exceeding one shilling and six pence per day each man", began to survey land to the North West of Navy Hall for a town.

Agreement for this survey had not been reached quickly. Over 3 years earlier, in August 1788, officials in Quebec had sent to Philip Frey, Jones' predecessor as Deputy Surveyor, a plan of a Town to be called Lenox, as well as instructions for its layout at a location on the banks of the Niagara River about 3 miles south of the river's mouth. However, the Loyalists of Niagara Township, too independent to be awed by instructions from a distant government, rejected the site, and so Frey was obliged to inform Quebec that "our community is as yet divided in opinion with respect to the place most fit for their town and public buildings. It seems to be the general opinion

it had better be voted for." And voted for it was, in the summer of 1790, at a series of special meetings of the militia arranged by a Land Board appointed to oversee the granting of tickets to lots. From four locations offered, the site chosen was a piece of Crown Land to the South East of Navy Hall. There matters stood until June 1791, when the Land Board, in accordance with instructions from Quebec, directed Augustus Jones "to proceed in laying out the town of Lenox."

There was yet another delay, when it was found that, because the Surveyor General's measurements were incorrect, the site would have to be moved to the North West of Navy Hall, an area "mostly covered with grain", noted the surveyor "which in a month or two will be gathered in." Having waited so long for approval, Jones decided he might as well wait for the harvest and thus it was that the first survey of the town did not begin until November 1791.

By December 5th, the Land Board was able to announce a draw for town lots 1 to 84 inclusive—the charge 25 shillings per acre, levied "for the purpose of defraying part of the expense of the jail or other Public Buildings". In addition to the Jail, two other "properties" specifically mentioned by the Board were a Public House and a Mason's Lodge and land for all three was duly set aside in a prime location near the water.* Ignored at first were the priorities stipulated by the Government—a cemetery, a common school, a church and a parsonage.

* The Public House known as the Yellow House was built on the lot now occupied by the Old Bank House, the Masonic Lodge on the present Lodge lot and the jail on the corner of Prideaux opposite the Lodge.

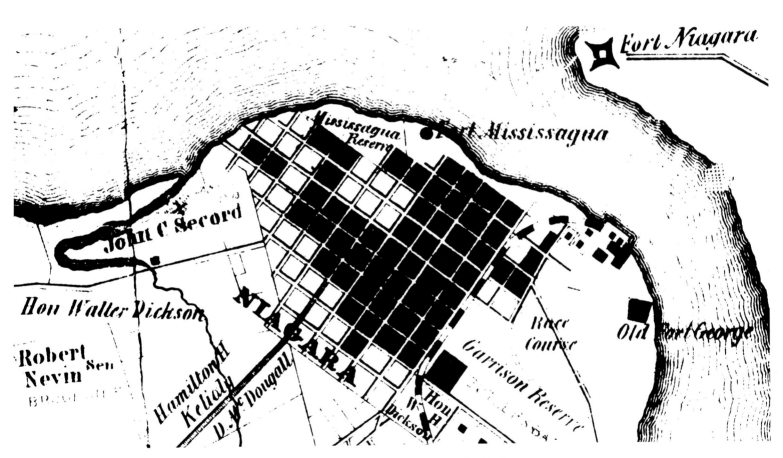

Location of Niagara-on-the-Lake

Nevertheless, basically the 1791 plan followed the Surveyor General's design of 4 acre blocks divided into one acre lots (except in the area between Queen and the lake where blocks were divided into ½ acre lots) with streets at right angles forming a grid pattern. Major streets were 99′ (1½ chains) wide, secondary streets 66′ wide. A town centre proposed for the block delineated by William, Mary, Mississauga and Butler streets was ignored by the townsfolk who chose their own centre near the water. However, William, Mary, Mississauga and Butler, remained like King and Queen streets, 99′ wide. By 1794, the town "plot" contained 412 surveyed lots, the last numbered being at the corner of King Street just south of Anne Street. Lots in this first-surveyed part of town retain their original numbers today.

The survey had little immediate impact on the development of the town—called Lenox by the government in Quebec, but Niagara by just about everyone else. When Hon. Peter Russell arrived nine days after Lieut. Governor Simcoe's entourage in the Fall of 1792 he complained that the Simcoes were living in tents and that there were "but three houses that are habitable—Dr. Kerr's, Mr. Dixon's (sic) and Mr. Addison's."*

It was Simcoe's choice of the town (which he renamed Newark, an appellation that matched Lenox on the popularity scale) as the first Capital of Upper Canada and the subsequent arrival first of government officials and soldiers and then of townspeople who moved in to provide services that changed the face of the village.

In 1795 the Duc de Rochefoucauld wrote that there were about 100 houses in Niagara most of them

superior to those in Kingston. Probably most significant was D.W. Smith's grand Georgian house, an 80′ × 40′ mansion with 4 fireplaces, built facing King Street on the 4 acre block known later as the "Market Square"; but plans of "Springfield", Peter Russell's estate, indicate that it was almost as impressive. There were levees at the refurbished Navy Hall, subscription balls and whist parties, races at the Turf Club, and stores catering to "fine" tastes—a silversmith, a purveyor of fine leather, a wine and tea outlet, an early apothecary. Newark—Niagara had blossomed almost overnight. Small wonder then, that when Simcoe ordered the capital and therefore the Legislature moved to York, a position deemed less vulnerable to American attack, his officials were, almost to a man, reluctant to exchange the comforts and amenities of the established town for the privations of the muddy backwater across the Lake. Many of them retained their Niagara residences and commuted to York by boat.

Though no longer the capital at the end of the 18th century, the town continued to grow. The military presence remained at the newly built Fort George, the town was still the county seat and Niagara's merchants continued to prosper. Principal suppliers for much of the province, they shipped out local produce—flour, salted meat, butter, cheese, potash—from farms in the township, and they imported books, tea, liquor, tobacco, yard goods and other finery. Newspapers of the day indicate that a far greater variety of 'useful' goods was for sale in the town of 1799 than in that of 1989.

Several reports of eyewitnesses in the 5 or 6 years before the war of 1812-14 (THE war in Niagara) extol the virtues of the town, its handsome houses, its

* Records suggest that Addison's town house was at the corner of Front and Victoria streets and that Mr. Dickson's was on Military Reserve land near the foot of King Street. Dr. Kerr's house was on Prideaux. Part of its basement has remained under Demeath.

two churches, its fruit trees, its twenty dry goods stores, its six taverns.

All this was torched by American troops aided by a traitorous group known as the Canadian Volunteers on December 10, 1813 and the town's residents, mostly women and children, were driven out into the snow.

The town that rose from the ashes of that cruel day contains within its boundaries no early pre-war homes or stores. Nevertheless, the legacy of the early Loyalists remains. To them we owe three vital components of Niagara's attractiveness. The town's location at the South East end of Lake Ontario adjacent to the mouth of the river, its wide streets, and the open space of the Fort George common.

At the end of the war, the government recommended relocation of the town away from the guns of Fort Niagara and accordingly extended its boundaries to include land at the South end of King Street. There on a piece of land donated by William Dickson, the town built a new Court House and Gaol, a two-storey structure considered one of the best of Upper Canada's early Court Houses. The handsome building inspired several builders to imitate its arcaded brickwork; but it lured very few residents away from the water.

This time the townsfolk did not demand to vote on the government's recommendation. They simply ignored it. A few rebuilt on former basements, more rebuilt on former sites; and most rebuilt in the part of town that had always been most populated—the "danger zone" bounded by Front, Simcoe, Johnson and King streets. Houses still surviving from this early post-war period (all changed to varying degrees) include the Old Bank House on Front Street, the Masonic Lodge, Demeath, the Promenade House, the Muirhead and Hiscott houses on Prideaux, the Wilson House and the Frey Cottage on Victoria Street; the Vanderlip and Greenlees houses on Johnson, the MacMonigle House on Gate Street and the Crysler-McDougal house on Queen Street. The land round the 1816-17 Court House, on the other hand, remained not much built on until the 1840's when many Irish immigrants, fleeing the potato famine, came to Niagara looking for work on the second Welland Canal and built in "Irish Town" where land was cheap.

A second extension of the town's boundaries took place in 1822-23 as a result of a land swap negotiated in order to keep the land around Fort Mississauga* free from buildings that might afford cover to an enemy. Owner of the land at the new Fort, James Crooks, a one-time bookbinder whose real talent seems to have been property development, exchanged his acreage for 21¼ acres east of King Street. Hence the streets that extend into Crooks "New Survey" beyond King have different names from those between King and Mississauga Streets. One acre at the corner of Simcoe and Queen was excluded from the exchange. This exclusion accounts for the unique position of the Richardson-Kiely house (#209 Queen Street) at the edge of the golf course.

Mr. Crooks did not have to wait long for buyers for his New Survey land. In the 1830's the early post-war building "boom" was invigorated by the formation of the Niagara Harbour and Dock Co., an enterprise that, in 1832-3, pumped out and excavated part of the marshy area near the mouth of the Niagara

---

* newly built in 1814 on a point further away from American guns than Fort George.

River (an area incidentally very close to the site of the 18th century Fairchild Shipyard) to make a basin 14′ deep.

The company spent about 20,000 pounds building a launching ramp, shops, and warehouses, much of it borrowed money. By 1838 it employed about 400 men some of them ship's carpenters who built houses that still display evidence of their wood-working skills. Between 1833 and 1840 the population of the town more than doubled and more stores were built on Queen Street to take care of the increase in business.

However, the opening of the Second Welland Canal in the mid 1840's made obsolete the old portage route round the Falls, a route vital to Niagara, and thus it signaled the end of the town's period of "working class prosperity". The Niagara Harbour and Dock Company, sinking under its debt, launched its last steamer in 1847.

The same year in a desperate attempt to retain its position as the headquarters of Lincoln County, the town built a brand new Court House and in 1854 town fathers loaned Samuel Zimmerman's Erie and Ontario Railroad 25,000 pounds to extend the rail line from Chippawa to the wharf. It was all in vain—Zimmerman died in a railway accident and St. Catharines became the county seat.

The boom was definitely over.

Some tangible evidence of the days when the dock area fueled the economy of the town remains. In the dock area itself, there's the Whale Inn, built c.1835 to cater to sailors, part of the Harbour Inn built somewhat later by one of the owners of the railway car factory, the railway right of way—now a grassy track along the river's edge, the Yacht basin

and the dock company's warehouse, now the Niagara Sailing Club Headquarters. On the main street 14 buildings have been identified as structures built between 1830 and 1850*. In other areas of town, many houses from this period survive.

In the last decade of the 19th century Niagara again experienced a revival based this time on the railway, the lake boats, and summer holiday trade. The town had invested its $8,000 compensation for the loss of the county seat in a "posh" hotel that was built on the bluffs at the foot of Regent Street. Opened in 1869, the Queen's Royal (not its first name) developed into a popular resort for long-term summer visitors. The hotel's bowling green, tennis courts, and golf course, its elegant sitting and dining rooms and its smartly uniformed bellhops became renowned across the continent. Many who came to the Queen's, fell in love with the Old Town and established their own summer houses in Niagara. Some, mostly Americans, bought and restored big old houses—like Randwood and its John Street neighbour, Pinehurst. Others built new houses—huge frame buildings with elaborate verandahs and often with turreted roofs on large lots facing the Mississauga Common. Once again Niagara had estates almost as grand as those of the late 18th century.

This first tourist boom had, at first, a leisurely gentle quality. Visitors sat on verandahs in rocking chairs, fished from row boats, or picnicked in Simcoe Park or at Paradise Grove, a well-treed spot on

* Greaves Jams (#55), the Old Bakery (#59), Marlene's Creative Vine (#135), The Open Cupboard (#4-8), the Owl and the Pussy Cat (#16), The Sherlock Block (#34-36), The Celtic Shop (#38-42), The Dee-LeDoux building (#54-58), The Old Greaves' House (#80), the former McClelland Store (#106), The old Gollop House (#118), the Evans Block (#122-124), as well as the Moffatt Inn on Picton St. and the house next to it at #66.

the river bank above Fort George. A few perhaps ate ice cream at Niagara's lone ice cream emporium where Mrs. Swift sold the homemade variety. The pace began to quicken somewhat after the turn of the century when four lake boats each made two crossings a day from Toronto and five Michigan Central Railway trains arrived daily from Buffalo. By late 1910 headlines in the Times newspaper were proclaiming "A Boom is On" and "Prospects are Bright for Old Niagara."

World War I interrupted the summer trade but troops stationed on the Common spent money in town and restaurants and several theatres including the present Royal George and a little theatre in the Court House were opened to cater to them. By May 1915, according to the Times, "The number of refreshment places in town when all are running, including the camp canteen and drug stores but excluding hotels" was twelve.

After the war, the automobile took its toll on the summer trade and the town slept. Restaurants and theatres closed and first the Queen's Royal and then the Oban and the Prince of Wales went bankrupt. Cows grazed peacefully on the Common. The local grocer's installation of a new electric scale and the baker's purchase of a truck rated announcements in the newspaper. However, there was activity beneath the surface calm. Rum running, in particular, provided entertaining tales, as well as excitement. There were also spirited arguments about the form and location of the War Memorial. Like their 18th century forebears, residents decided that this subject "had better be voted for". The Clock Tower, designed by Charles Wilmot and built in 1922, was the result of the vote. Circa 1937, the pro-

vince undertook the reconstruction of Fort George and pumped some much needed money into the economy, but very few had enough cash to erect new buildings or to refurbish old ones.

World War II came and went, leaving ridges on the golf course where troops had practiced rifle drills, additional names of those who had sacrificed their lives on the Clock Tower, and a block of veterans' houses in the Castlereagh, Davy, Nelles, King area. However, fortunately the post World War II boom did not immediately give rise to a spate of tearing down and rebuilding in Old Niagara. There was a "breathing space" of several years. Then in the late 1950's there came a recognition that Niagara's heritage was its greatest asset. The late Mrs. Kathleen Drope saved a cluster of old homes from destruction, among them the Greenlees, and MacMonigle houses and Slave Cottage at the Gate—Johnson corner. The Oppenheimers, of Buffalo, restored several buildings including the Whale Inn, at the foot of King Street. And Frank Hawley, a member of the first Board of the Ontario Heritage Foundation, saw the potential in the neglected Breakenridge House at the corner of William and Mississauga and restored it to its original magnificence. The Niagara Foundation and its President Gerry Wooll, Dr. Stokes, whose "Old Niagara on the Lake" published in 1971 remains the definitive study of the town's architecture, the Parker family who have maintained the Wilderness as it was, John Downton, Paul Firlotte, Ron Gordon and the late Paul Johns have also been instrumental in the cause of preservation. The town itself got into the act making the renovation of the 1847 Court House its Bicentennial project in 1981, and commissioning a Heritage Conservation District plan in 1986. Plans are already afoot to expand the Heritage District.

One of the cornerstones of the town's latest period of growth and prosperity has been the Shaw Festival Theatre, launched by Brian Doherty in 1962 on a makeshift stage in the Court House. In 1973 the Festival Theatre was built on the corner of the Commons though not without a lengthy debate among townsfolk about the appropriateness of the site. The theatre brought a new vitality to the town. Moreover some who came to see a play, like those who came to the Queen's Royal a century ago, fell in love with the town and bought and restored older homes. Others have built new houses, not always 'sympathetic' to their surroundings.

Not all tourists are theatre goers. There are other interests to pursue—the town's architecture, art galleries, museums, golf course, and its main street stores, now largely boutiques or ice cream and frozen yogurt stores catering to the tourist trade. The change in function and often in identity of the main street stores and the building of large hotels in town have provoked a controversy that has been well reported in the media and that became a major issue in the municipal election of 1988.

The voters issued a preliminary verdict on the legacy of the current boom by returning a majority of councillors who expressed concern for heritage. The final verdict must await the judgement of time.

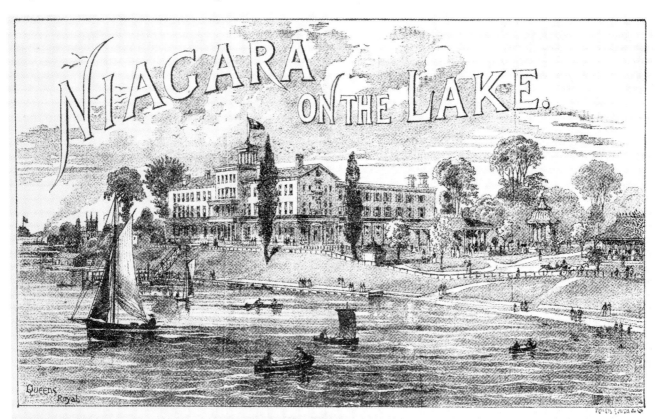

QUEEN'S ROYAL HOTEL.

Opening of the First Parliament of Upper Canada.

Painting by J.D. Kelly
Confederation Life, Toronto

Lieutenant-Governor Simcoe opened the first Parliament at Newark (Niagara-on-the-Lake) on September 17, 1792.

There is some controversy as to where the first Parliament of Upper Canada actually convened. According to various records, the meeting could have been held at a specially-erected tent located either on the hill, at Butler's Barracks, at the Indian Council House, at the Freemason's Hall or, most probably, at the Navy Hall as it has been depicted in the painting of J.D. Kelly.

The opening of the first Parliament was marked by a colourful ceremony. Members of the 26th Regiment from Fort Niagara formed the honour guard. There was a band and a colour guard, and Butler's Rangers and the Queen's Rangers provided the military escort.

THE FIRST PROVINCIAL PARLIAMENT 1792

On September 17, 1792, Colonel John Graves Simcoe, Lieutenant-Governor of Upper Canada, opened in this community, then the capital, the first provincial parliament. The legislature consisted of an appointed Legislative Council and an elected Legislative Assembly. Its opening marked the introduction of a form of representative government into this province. Previously, both the French and British regimes had been directed by a royal governor advised by an appointed council of officials and prominent citizens. This first parliament held all its sittings in "Newark", as Simcoe had re-named Niagara, but the second was summoned to meet in 1797 at York (Toronto), the new seat of government.

Archaeological and Historic Sites Board of Ontario.

Fort George.

Painting by E. Walsh
PAC-C26

The first Fort George was built between 1796 and 1799. Situated on the west bank of the Niagara River, approximately one mile from Lake Ontario, the post was constructed to replace Fort Niagara, which the British were forced to evacuate in 1796 under the terms of Jay's Treaty. Far from being an imposing work, the first Fort George consisted of six small bastions connected by a line of cedar picketing and surrounded by a shallow dry ditch. During the War of 1812 all wooden buildings were destroyed, and only a stone powder magazine remained.

Fort George officers' mess.

Parks Canada

The fort was originally intended to command the Lake Ontario entrance to the Niagara River and protect the town of Niagara-on-the-Lake, but it was located too far from the entrance of the river to be effective.

On May 27, 1813, the Americans launched a major bombardment in an assault on Fort George. The British post was levelled completely by the fire from Fort Niagara and an American contingent of 6,000 men advanced upon the defenders under cover of the morning mist. After a gallant fight the British under Brigadier General John Vincent were forced to evacuate the fort.

Fort George, marching exercise.

Parks Canada

The original Fort George was reconstructed following an agreement in the mid-1930's between the federal and provincial governments to share the cost of the project. Begun in 1937, the fort was completed in 1940, although the official opening was delayed until after World War II.

The bodies of General Isaac Brock, hero of the Battle of Queenston Heights, and his aide-de-camp John MacDonell were originally buried at Fort George. However, in 1824 they were removed to a vault beneath the newly-constructed memorial on Queenston Heights, overlooking the site where the battle was fought and where Brock was killed. A stone now marks the site of their original graves.

Fort George, officers' dining room.

The officers' dining room was the centre of social activities, and officers expected to live like gentlemen even on the frontier. Each table was equipped with silverware, fine china, pewter serving dishes and after-dinner decanters of port and sherry.

One of Butler's Barracks, corner of King and John streets.

The original log barracks were constructed in 1779 near Fort George by Lieutenant-Colonel John Butler to house his Rangers and their families. During the War of 1812 some of these barracks were burned down or destroyed by American gunfire.

Shortly after the war, the British Army decided to replace the barracks, selecting a new location at the corner of King and John streets, a safer place out of range of the American artillery.

Between the end of the war and towards the 1850's, twenty permanent buildings were constructed to serve British regulars and Canadian Militia. When British troops left Canada after Confederation, the responsibility of defending the country was assumed by the Canadian government which utilized the barracks as part of a training area centre.

As time passed, some of the buildings deteriorated, and now only four barracks remain. Restored by Parks Canada they house a static display of the military development in Canada from early days to the present.

Butler's Burying Ground, Butler Street.

The historic plaque erected by the Ontario Heritage Foundation, and the Ministry of Culture and Recreation at Butler's burying ground reads as follows:

> Lieutenant-Colonel John Butler, 1725-96.—Born in Connecticut, this well-known Loyalist soldier and pioneer settler in the Niagara area obtained a large tract of land in the Mohawk Valley, N.Y. He was commissioned in the Seven Years' War. Forfeiting his estate at the outbreak of the American Revolution, he raised a Loyalist corps, "Butler's Rangers", which was the scourge of the rebel-held territory in New York State. The unit was disbanded in 1784, and led by their former commander, many settled in the Niagara Peninsula.

On September 17, 1792, Colonel John Butler was among the distinguished guests at the opening of the first Parliament of Upper Canada at Niagara-on-the-Lake, known then as Newark.

Butler's graveyard plaques, Butler Street.

Next to Butler's grave, on the left side, is Butler's Burying Ground. Some of those buried there are: Thomas Butler, died December 12, 1812; Ann, wife of Thomas Butler, died April 15, 1842; Thomas Butler Jr., died December 14, 1848; Butler Muirhead, died November 29, 1824; James Muirhead, died March 24, 1834; Deborah Freel, died February 12, 1816; Jane, wife of Robert Rist, died October 31, 1831; Maria Caroline, wife of Major Richardson, died August 16, 1845; Eliza, wife of Charles Richardson died September 22, 1833; and infant daughter of Charles and Eliza Richardson, Eliza Magdalene, died June 4, 1828; Ralfe Clench, died January 19, 1828; Mary E., wife of John Gustavus Stevenson, and daughter of James and Jane Butler, died May, 1854.

Navy Hall, on the shore of the Niagara River.

The origin of Navy Hall can be traced to the year 1765 when over-crowding at Fort Niagara necessitated the construction of new barracks on the west side of the Niagara River. Built by naval artificers, they were located near the same site on which the present Navy Hall stands.

In the years to follow, the site became a complex of various buildings designated for storage, repair shops, offices and living quarters for the officers of the Navy Department serving on Lake Ontario. When John Graves Simcoe, the first Lieutenant-Governor of Upper Canada, arrived in 1792, he changed the name of the community to Newark and on September 17, 1792, he may have opened there the first Parliament of Upper Canada. The Simcoes lived in tents beside the river until the buildings at the Navy Hall complex had been repaired and refurbished for their use. After his departure to England, the Navy Hall was used as a storehouse and then as barracks.

In time the barracks were abandoned and left to fall into ruins, until restored in 1911 as a military training camp. After World War I it was once more abandoned, only to be rescued again in 1930 by the Government of Ontario. In the reconstruction, wood from other buildings was used and the walls were covered with stone.

The Simcoe Monument, Navy Hall.

Facing the long stone building known as Navy Hall which overlooks the Niagara River, is a massive monument erected in honour of Lieutenant Governor John Graves Simcoe and his wife Elizabeth.

When Simcoe returned to England in 1781 following the strenuous days of the American Revolution, his physician advised him to assume a quiet life and take care of himself. Simcoe decided to visit friends who were delighted to welcome him.

While at Hembury Fort, some miles from Honiton, Simcoe decided to see his father's friends, Admiral and Mrs. Graves. Here in the summer of 1782 he met a young and beautiful girl with whom he fell in love. She was sixteen and he was thirty, but despite her youth the marriage took place on the 30th of December, 1782.

Appointed in 1791 as the first Lieutenant Governor of the new Province of Upper Canada, Simcoe arrived at Niagara on July 26, 1792 after voyaging from Kingston where he had taken his oath of office.

During his stay at Niagara, Simcoe changed the town's name to Newark. Mrs. Simcoe, an accomplished artist, made many sketches of local scenery.

Fort Mississauga, Queen Street North.

PAC. Watercolour by Armstrong

Fort Mississauga on Mississauga Point was built in 1814 by military labour, out of the rubble of the town of Niagara, frontier settlement and first capital of Upper Canada which was burned to the ground by American forces in the War of 1812. Constructed in the five-point star shape popular in the design of European forts at the time, the fort was to replace the first Fort George at Niagara which, according to contemporary description, was "tumbling into ruins".

The fort was to secure the Niagara River and serve as a base for naval operations on Lake Ontario. By mid-summer of 1814, work had progressed to the point that ditching and picketing as well as two bomb-proof magazines and two furnaces were completed and the brick tower and splinter-proof barracks were under construction.

The fort continued to be occupied from time to time as a military post until 1845 and again was utilized briefly by the military during the Fenian troubles in 1866 and 1870. After that, the fort was left to fall into ruin.

Clock Tower, Queen Street.

The red brick and gray limestone tower which stands in the centre of Queen Street facing the Court House was unveiled with suitable ceremony on June 23, 1922 to commemorate the soldiers of the town who fell in World War I. The names of these soldiers are inscribed on a special tablet.

The ceremony was performed by the Lieutenant-Governor of Ontario, H. Cockshutt, attended by Mayor and Mrs. Mussen, Rev. C.M.E. Smith, rector of St. Mark's Church, local dignitaries and hundreds of spectators.

In 1947 the names of the town's fallen soldiers from World War II were added, and in 1958 a clock purchased in England was installed replacing the original clock. The clock tower is a famous town landmark.

Niagara Apothecary, Queen Street.

Located at 5 Queen Street, the Niagara Apothecary is the oldest pharmacy in Ontario. Its beginning dates back to 1820, when a chemist from Wales named Evans established his business in the community.

In 1865 Henry Paffard purchased the building, which was previously the office of Judge E.C. Campbell. After the building was enlarged and renovated, Mr. Paffard moved his business, which had been located a couple of doors away, to this address. Besides being a good druggist, Mr. Paffard was also a popular mayor, elected several times to represent his community.

Prior to the 1860's, the building sat back from the street and had a verandah across its front with an entrance reached via a short flight of stairs. Henry Paffard lowered the building and extended it to the street line when he moved his business to this address. From 1866 to 1964, the building was used continuously as a pharmacy in succession by Paffard, John de Witt Randall, A.J. Coyne and E.W. Field.

The Niagara Apothecary and the Golden Mortar, Queen Street.

Above the entry door, on the panelled wall, hangs the Golden Mortar, the ancient symbol of pharmacists. On both sides of the door are two large Italianate windows which offer a clear view inside the store. After Mr. Field's death, the Niagara Foundation purchased the building to save it from destruction.

In 1970 the building underwent a major restoration, sponsored by the Heritage Foundation, the Historic Sites Branch of the Federal Department of Indian Affairs and the Ontario College of Pharmacy.

On Friday, May 14, 1971, the Niagara Apothecary was officially reopened to the public.

The Niagara Apothecary, Queen Street

The spacious apothecary is furnished circa 1866. On the wooden shelves stand various sizes of medicine jars, brass mortars and medical scales. Each jar, labelled in latin, contains some medicine.

At the rear on top of the medicine cupboard there is a large clock enclosed by intricate wood carvings. Despite its considerable age the clock functions perfectly. Behind the original black walnut counter stands an attendant who answers questions concerning the early days of pharmacy.

The Sign of the Pineapple, 16 Queen Street.

Noted for its tall, narrow facade, its pineapple symbol and its Gothic Revival store front, the Sign of the Pineapple was built circa 1830 on land leased from the town's market commissioners.

Though in recent years it has housed a toy shop, for most of its life it was a grocery store. Ownership passed from Steve Follett to Fred Best Jr., Dick Allen, Fred Matthews, then H. Reid and Son, all purveyors of food.

The third storey has served various functions including storage, a lodge room (of the United Workmen) and a little theatre.

The Gothic Revival store front is not original. It was added in the 1970's as a sympathetic substitute for a shop front that had been destroyed to make garage doors for a penny arcade that occupied the building briefly.

The Angel Inn, 46 Market Street

The Angel Inn was built on part of a four-acre block owned by D.W. Smith, Simcoe's Deputy Surveyor General and builder of what was probably the finest of Niagara's pre-war houses. After Smith returned to England his four acres became first Crown and then town property, leased to individual merchants by market commissioners.

In 1826 Richard Howard leased or purchased this "excellent tavern and stand known as the Sign of the Angel Inn" from John Ross, who was probably its first owner, and operated it until he purchased the Promenade House in 1845. John Fraser, who had a sail-making business at the dock, bought the inn from Howard, perhaps because work at the dock was getting slow, and changed its name to Mansion House and then to Fraser's Hotel.

The two-storey timber-framed building with its rather unusual asymmetrical front is to-day known by its original name.

The Court House, Queen Street.

Architect William Thomas designed Niagara's third Court House, built in 1847 as part of the town's effort to remain the seat of government of Lincoln County. Two Niagara craftsmen, mason John Thornton and carpenter John Davidson, were sub-contractors.

In 1861 Niagara lost the County seat to its more rapidly growing neighbour, St. Catharines, and so the Court House became the Town Hall. From time to time it housed the Post Office, a bank, a little theatre, a fire hall, and market (at the rear) and even a suspender-making operation. Today it contains the library, the Shaw's Court House Theatre and Parks Canada offices as well as the Lord Mayor's Reception Chamber.

Restoration of the building, including replacing the cupola, was the town's bicentennial project.

Sherlock Block, 34-36 Queen Street.

The building is dated circa 1850 but derives its popular name from Stephen Sherlock, one of its 20th century owners. Over the years it has housed a variety of businesses, including Bishop's grocery and butcher shop, a bakery, an undertaker's, a newspaper office and a pool room.

A picture of the street circa 1870 shows the building with seven narrow windows at the second storey level, two (or possibly even three) doorways at the lower level and a canopy marked with the words CASH STORE overhanging the street. The gable is a later addition.

Daly-Alma Store, 44-46 Queen Street.

The Old Niagara Bookshop and the Cameron Jeffries Store.

Reconstructed in 1981 on the site of the former Daly-Alma Store, circa 1825, this building was the winner of an Ontario Renews Award.

The multitude of beautiful stores, restaurants and boutiques make Queen Street a favourite meeting place for thousands of visitors who congregate from various areas of Canada and different corners of the United States. It is estimated that each year approximately 3 million tourists attend the famous Shaw Festival Theatre, visit the historic museums, take pictures of the well-kept houses and enjoy the atmosphere of genial hospitality.

The growing interest in Niagara-on-the-Lake is phenomenal. Last year the Chamber of Commerce responded to over 4,000 inquiries concerning the town and the area's points of historical interest.

The Dee Building, 54-58 Queen Street

In a letter to the *Niagara Times* (republished in a Niagara Historical Society pamphlet), Mr. James A. Davidson recalled that in 1836 James Lockhart operated a branch of the Commercial Bank in a two-storey brick store on this site. Lockhart leased the building from owner John Young, who in 1840 sold the property to William Dee, a merchant. In 1843 Dee raised a substantial mortgage on the property, suggesting extensive renovations or rebuilding.

By the spring of 1848, Dee had moved to Stamford and an "acre of ground on Queen St. upon which the store of Mr. D. Lockhart is situated together with a store occupied by Mr. W. Willson" was advertised for sale in the *Niagara Chronicle*.

The building has since served as a grocery and liquor store (Woodington-Bottomly 1893-1912), a bakery and a shoe store. F.B. LeDoux bought it from the administrators of the estate of Mrs. Bottomly (formerly Mrs. Woodington) in the 1940's.

The Rowley Block, circa 1890, Queen Street.

After fire destroyed part of the block on the north side of Queen Street opposite the Court House, Salmon Rowley, a gem jar manufacturer from Philadelphia, built this fine commercial building.

Bank of Montreal, Queen Street

The Bank of Montreal, built in 1975, harmonizes with the older buildings erected in previous years. Queen Street is a popular meeting place where people can shop, dine, watch their favourite shows and do their banking.

Squire Clements, Queen Street.

Originally known as "Squire Clements" store, for many years it was Connolly's store, housing an early ice cream parlour. The brick building on the right was the Fire Hall (1911).

McClelland's West End Store, 106 Queen Street.

Until very recently, this store with the great T sign on its facade had been a provisioners for over 150 years. Its earliest occupants, Lewis Clement who built it in the 1830's and Balfour and Drysdale and the Christie Brothers who leased it, were, like the McClellands who purchased it in 1873 and operated it for close to a century, purveyors of fine quality food. The McClellands' cheeses in particular become famous far beyond the confines of the town and the store itself became a Niagara landmark.

However, in the 1980's the fine food business became one of the "casualties" of the current "boom" in Niagara.

The upper facade of the building has retained most of its original detail; the lower portion with its recessed doorway flanked by cast iron columns is part of an 1880's "modernization" which included the addition of the building to the left.

MacMonigle House, 240 Gate Street.

Joseph Adnams, a carpenter and joiner sold ¼ acre of land at the corner of Johnson and Gate Streets to John MacMonigle, a yeoman, in 1816 and it may have been Adnams who built the nucleus of this house for MacMonigle. The property changed hands several times before being bought in 1839 by William Curtis, whose descendants retained it for close to a century.

Originally two rooms on the ground floor and one upstairs, the dwelling was extended to the south in the 1850's.

The house has been known by various names including "The Homestead", "The Shoemaker's Cottage", (William Curtis Jr. was a shoemaker) and "Granny Curtis' Cottage". Like its neighbour the Greenlees House on Johnson Street, it was restored by Mrs. Kathleen Drope.

122-124 Queen Street.

The timber frame building of Georgian proportions at the left is a well-preserved 1840's dwelling. To its right is an earlier circa 1825 building once used as a Customs House. The roof parapet was at one time surmounted by a coat of arms. Both buildings are set right to the street line.

The Royal George Theatre, Queen Street.

The Royal George Theatre traces its roots to the time of World War I when Mrs. Norris erected the building for the purpose of entertaining the troops. This was the first building in town constructed from a form of cement blocks. She called her establishment the "Kitchener".

The movie house, however, was not always successful. In 1919 Mrs. Norris tried to sell the building to the town to be converted into a Memorial Hall and used as a meeting place for boys and girls. When negotiations failed, George Reid purchased the building and after renovations renamed it the "Royal George".

Further changes to the building were made in the 1930's when John Allan became the proprietor. He changed its name to the "Brock". In 1946 the movie house was sold to Dewey McCourt and then in 1972 to Canadian Mime who changed the name back to the "Royal George". The new owners operated the theatre until 1978 and two years later the building was purchased by the Shaw Festival by then in its third stage of expansion.

118 Queen Street.

This side-gabled two-storey building of Georgian proportions, traditionally dated circa 1830, was probably built for Jacob Caniff, a Niagara watchmaker who sold the property to James A. Davidson in 1848. Davidson later recalled that in the mid-1830's Caniff's shop was one of several stores in this block. (His reminiscences are included in the Niagara Historical Society pamphlet #11). By the end of the 19th century, the building, like its neighbours to the northwest, had become a private residence. It was purchased by Samuel Hindle, a building contractor, in 1894 and by World War I veteran William Gollop, a blacksmith whose shop was in the barn at the rear in 1918.

For over a decade it has again, like its neighbours, functioned as a store.

The most notable feature of the building is the doorcase with a shelf-like cornice and ornamental pilasters flanking side lights.

The Rogers-Harrison House, 157 Queen Street

A *Niagara Gleaner* notice of July 4, 1817 announcing that "James Rogers has completed his large and commodious house on Queen Street" signalled the building of this fine dwelling. Much of Rogers' original exterior detail remains, the doorway with its side lights and fanlight being especially notable.

For a few years the property became a tavern, operated first by James' widowed mother Agnes and later by Charles Koune.

In 1833 a three-storey tin-roofed building constructed by James Blain was added at the corner to serve as a store. It was demolished many years ago.

The current owners of the house, the Harrison family, are descendants of Mary Ann Rogers, sister of James Rogers, who married John Blake circa 1837.

The MacDougal House, 165 Queen Street.

Ralph and Elizabeth Clench bought the half-acre lot in 1811 for 50 pounds and sold two-thirds of it in 1820 to Adam Crysler, the probable builder of the house, for 125 pounds. In 1849, Charles Crysler, Adam's heir, sold the house to Colonel Daniel Mac-Dougal after whom the house is generally named. MacDougal had been so severely wounded at Lundy's Lane that he was not expected to live. In fact, despite his wounds he lived to the ripe old age of 84. For many years he was the treasurer for Lincoln, Welland and Haldimand Counties and he owned several properties in town.

MacDougal's descendants occupied the house until well after the turn of the century and one of them, his grandson, Willie Newton, became well known both as a brilliant freelance journalist and an eccentric.

This well-preserved building with its distinctive double arcades and elaborate door-case is deservedly one of the most photographed residences in Niagara.

The Richardson-Kiely House, Heritage Inn, 209 Queen Street.

   The nucleus of the house, a five-bay structure with a striking centre doorway, was built in 1832 for Charles Richardson, M.P. for Niagara.

   In 1836, Richardson sold the property to James Lockhart, proprietor of a large dry goods store on Queen Street, ship owner and director of the Niagara Harbour and Dock Company (n.b. Lockhart Street in the dock area). Lockhart declared bankruptcy in 1846 and forfeited the house to Charles L. Hall, his legal advisor and neighbour across Simcoe Street.

   Circa 1899, Niagara builder John Ellison added the wing at the right for American businessman George K. Birge. In the 1960's Mrs. Kathleen Drope, whose efforts saved several early houses, lived in this house.

Burberry Cottage, circa 1840, 17 Prideaux Street.

For the last quarter of the 19th century, this neat dwelling on its small lot was the home of Misses Catherine Claus and Elizabeth Barbara Comer, who had purchased the property from Andrew and Sarah Carnochan.

Advertised for sale by Miss Comer's executors in April 1899, the house was described as having seven rooms. It was renovated in the 1960's.

28 Prideaux Street.

The nucleus of this house, built circa 1817 for Dr. James Muirhead on the site of a house burned in 1813, was owned for most of the 19th century by members of the Richards family, Muirhead's descendants. During that period it housed at least one well-known tenant, artist Francis Grainger. The original house has been considerably enlarged and altered.

31 Prideaux Street.

    Though the nucleus of this house was probably built for William Wilson in the 1840's, registry office records suggest that extensive renovations were made by Edward Thompson in the early 1870's. Thompson sold the house to Mary Ball Servos, granddaughter of Captain Bernard Frey.

    James Aikins, twice mayor of the town, bought the property from the Servos estate.

The Stewart House, 42 Prideaux Street.

In 1818, Augustus Jones, the first Surveyor of the town, sold this lot to Jemina Stewart, widow of Alexander Stewart, one of the first lawyers in Upper Canada.

The house, built about 1830, was occupied by a member of the Stewart family until the late 1860's. A later occupant was John Lees Alma, owner of Alma's Store at the corner of Queen and Regent streets.

The residence is notable for its five-bay arcaded facade, its elaborate doorcase and magnificent staircase. The original part of the building was only one room deep.

42 Prideaux Street
Stairway

42 Prideaux Street
Dining Room

42 Prideaux Street
The Parlour

The Promenade House, 55 Prideaux Street.

An elegant building with Flemish bond brickwork and a handsome transom, the Promenade House was one of Niagara's early hostelries.

Originally the property of Elizabeth Thomson, it was bought by John Breakenridge in 1822 and then by innkeeper David Botsford in 1826, who gave it its name. In 1845 the tavern was taken over by Richard Howard and became, according to one prominent lodger, "the most respectable inn in town".

At one time a long frame wing stretched down Regent Street in which Polish soldiers were lodged in 1917.

59 Prideaux Street.

This neat well-kept house, built for Don Sherlock in the late 1930's, is a good example of a relatively recent building that is sympathetic to the streetscape.

69 Prideaux Street, Demeath.

When Simcoe arrived in Niagara, the house on this lot, built for Dr. Robert Kerr, surgeon to the Indian Department and Grand Master of the Grand Masonic Lodge of Upper Canada, was said to have been one of only three decent houses in the village. Kerr's first house burned in 1813, but the old foundations under the present house built circa 1815 likely belonged to the earlier residence.

Hiscott House—78 Prideaux Street.

Known as the Hiscott House for its owner in the 1860's, Richard Hiscott, a prominent early land developer, the house was probably built for William McKean, circa 1817. The shed-roofed verandah and the rear wing are later additions.

Kirby House, 130 Front Street.

The most famous owner of this dwelling was William Kirby, author of *Annals of Niagara, the Golden Dog* and *Canadian Idylls.*

The house is dated circa 1818. However, the fact that its lot was one of those seized by the Commission for Forfeited Estates in 1822 suggests that there was no building at that date. A carpenter named Thomas Courtney who acquired the land in 1832 may have been the builder and it was his son Thomas Jr. who sold part of the lot with the house to William Kirby in 1857. The deed stipulated that Kirby and Courtney would share a well on the property.

The doorcase is perhaps the building's most notable original feature. The French windows, a mid-19th century alteration, indicate that Kirby added a verandah to the house.

The Oban Inn, Front Street

A small house built by Mary Trumble circa 1822 was enlarged in the 1860's and named the Oban House by Lake boat Captain Duncan Milloy who died there in 1871 at the age of 46. In July 1895 his son, Captain W.A. Milloy opened his residence as a private hotel and it was renamed the Oban Inn. Over time it has been further enlarged and during World War I served as an officers' mess when troops were occupying the present-day golf course.

A quarter mile east is Fort Mississauga, built in 1814 from the rubble of houses destroyed in the War of 1812, and the bricks of the lighthouse that once stood here.

Guests at the Inn enjoy the panorama provided by Lake Ontario and the view of Fort Niagara.

26 Front Street.

The house was built circa 1910 for William Black, caretaker of the Queen's Royal Hotel, a popular resort that stood on the bluffs at the foot of Regent Street from 1869 to the 1930's.

Behind this 1910 house can be seen a very early building, possibly moved to the site from across the street.

10 Front Street.

Built circa 1817 for Thomas Racey, a town warden, the house was later owned by Thomas McCormick, agent for the Bank of Upper Canada—hence its popular name "The Old Bank House". The verandah is a Victorian addition but some of the old sash remains, as do parts of a vault in the basement.

St. Vincent de Paul Roman Catholic Church, Picton Street.

In April 1831, "a meeting of the Catholic inhabitants of Niagara" chaired by Daniel McDougal, agreed that money should be collected in order to build a Catholic church in the town.

St. Vincent de Paul, begun in 1834 on four acres of military reserve land, was the result of that "building campaign".

In 1965 the original building was enlarged by the addition of a nine-sided front section with full-length Gothic windows and three sets of oak doors. The original clapboard sheeting has been replaced with stucco.

St. Mark's Anglican Church, Byron Street.

The first St. Mark's, constructed between 1804 and 1810, was used as a barracks and hospital during the 1812-14 war. Only its stone walls survived the fire of December, 1813. Reconstruction began in 1816 and the new church was consecrated on August 3, 1828 by the Bishop of Quebec. In 1843 transepts and chancel were added to take care of the growing congregation and the formerly rectangular building became cruciform.

The church's first rector, Rev. Robert Addison, delivered the prayer at the opening of the first parliament of Upper Canada in September 1792. He served the parish for 37 years, until his death in 1829.

St. Mark's Church
The Lectern

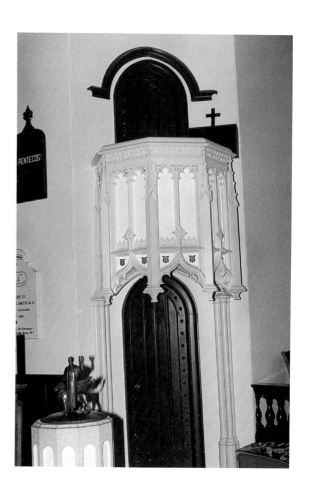

St. Mark's Church
The Pulpit

The Rectory—17 Byron Street.

The Anglican rectory, the only Tuscan Villa in town, was built in 1858, a year after the arrival of Archdeacon MacMurray, third rector of St. Mark's.

Notable features of the building are the panelled chimneys, the wide eaves supported by ornamental brackets, the square tower with small balconies and the pressed buff brick.

The Moffat Inn, 60 Picton Street.

Richard Moffat built this inn in 1835 on a quarter acre of James Crook's New Survey land.

Moffat's Inn and its neighbour to the west at the corner of Davy Street catered to travelers associated with the Niagara Harbour and Dock Co. In W.H. Smith's Gazette of 1848 this inn and Howard's (the Promenade House) were described as the two best taverns in Niagara.

After Richard Moffat's death his widow Mary hired Jimmy Doyle to work in the inn for $4 a month. Doyle eventually acquired both the Moffat and its neighbour. Only the Moffat survives today. The hotel's central entrance is relatively new but the building's fine Georgian proportions remain as a record of Moffat's simple good taste.

Campbell House, 24 Platoff Street.

This house may have been built in the late 1860's. Located in the New Survey area, it is situated next to the Dover-Daly Cottage and the Malcolmson House. Younger than these two, it could have been built by Robert Carnathan, keeper of the Moffat Inn at one time.

The Dover House, 20 Platoff Street.

Both #16 and #20 are built on New Survey land that James Crooks sold to Henry Sewell, a carpenter, in 1835.

Sewell subdivided the land in 1838, selling the easterly portion (No. 20) to Thomas Dover and the westerly part (No. 16) to Peter Baikie.

No. 20, a small board and batten salt box, is usually ascribed to Thomas Dover. However, two other carpenters bought the property, Edward Dixon in 1842 and Thomas Eedson in 1844, and either or both of them may have also had a hand in the building.

The Malcolmson House, 16 Platoff Street.

No. 16 may have been started by Baikie before he sold the property to James Malcolmson in 1841 and moved to Davy Street. However, Malcolmson is generally credited with this building, a simple clapboard dwelling with a well-balanced facade.

Malcolmson, Dixon, Eedson and Sewell were all charter members of the Niagara Mechanics Institute established to promote "Scientific pursuits, the advancement of knowledge and the acquisition of a library" and in 1852 Eedson was elected treasurer and librarian. The institute's name was eventually changed to the Public Library.

The Old Public School, Platoff Street.

From 1859 when it was built by master mason John Thornton until 1948 when Parliament Oak School on King Street opened, this was Niagara's Public School.

The sturdy old structure, its exterior still largely unchanged, now contains apartments.

Niagara Historical Society Museum, 43 Castlereagh Street.

When the Niagara Historical Society was formed in December 1895, its objects were to encourage the study of Canadian history and literature, to build Canadian loyalty and patriotism and to collect and safely preserve Canadian historical records and relics. To speed matters along, each member was asked to give or loan documents or relics to the Society. A need for a "historical room" was soon felt as the members responded.

In May 1896, the Town donated for their use, the Grand Jury Room on the third floor of the Niagara Court House. (The site today is the balcony of the Court House Theatre.)

The collection grew rapidly due partly to the enthusiam of its founders, Janet Carnochan, the Society's first President for 30 years, and William Kirby, the Honorary President. Both were collectors in the true Victorian sense in that they assembled anything old or said to be old regardless of its relevance to Niagara or Canadian history. A case of stuffed birds, a Cuban machete, a table cover made of soldiers' coats from the Crimean War, a Roman battle axe and a U.S. Colonel's military coat from the Civil War: all were displayed in the Historical Room. With such eclectic tastes and generous patrons, the collection soon outgrew the Grand Jury Room.

Niagara Historical Society Museum
43 Castlereagh Street.

The Town continued to support the Society by permitting them to display their artifacts in the Town Hall during the summers of 1905 and 1906. This arrangement was not satisfactory as twice a year there was the labor of moving a growing collection of fragile articles. It became obvious that the Society needed their own building to house their collection.

A vigorous building campaign was launched, and under the determined and devoted leadership of the Society's president, Janet Carnochan, sufficient funds were gathered. By April 1906 construction began under the supervision of its architect, W.B. Allan, of St. Catharines. He had the distinction of designing the first museum building in Ontario and Memorial Hall is one of the main buildings still used for displays in the present-day museum.

The building was officially opened on June 4, 1907, by the Lieutenant-Governor of Ontario, Sir Mortimer Clark, and was dedicated to the memory of United Empire Loyalists who settled and defended Niagara.

The emphasis on the contribution made to Canada by the Loyalists was reflected in the collection. Although almost a hundred years had passed, artifacts from the War of 1812 and even earlier were donated and still form the most important part of the museum collection. Brock's hat was donated by a descendant of a Loyalist.

In 1926, Janet Carnochan died but so well did she lay the foundations for the museum that it remained a vital institution in the community. During these years, school visits were encouraged as students from the nearby Grammar School (the town's High School) visited the museum.

JANET CARNOCHAN · 1839-1926
BORN at Stamford, C.W. Educated at Niagara. Principal of Public School 1872-78
Teacher in High School 1878-1900. Secretary of Public Library 1891-1920.
Founder of Niagara Historical Society 1895 and its President till 1920. Curator of
this Museum. Author of History of Niagara and of many pamphlets on local
Historical subjects
EAM DVXIT AMOR PATRIAE

Janet Carnochan

In 1950, a new high school was built and the Town, in its tradition of supporter, donated the old Grammar School building to the Niagara Historical Society. For some years, the collection was housed in the two buildings, but this proved impractical. In 1972, another building campaign was launched, and the two buildings were linked by a wing. To complement the historic buildings, eight windows from the old parish hall of St. Mark's Church were placed in the wing.

The Museum buildings are historically designated by the Province of Ontario and supported by the Town of Niagara-on-the-Lake, the Province of Ontario and the Niagara Historical Society as well as by private donors.

The collection is rare in that it has a large number of pre-Victorian artifacts. Recently, the Museum received the Servos collection. Over 250 artifacts illustrate the domestic life in the early 19th century. These include military uniforms, kitchen utensils, and documents.

The Niagara Historical Society is proud of the heritage of its town as the first capital of Upper Canada and Loyalist settlement. However, the history of Niagara-on-the-Lake did not end with the burning of the town in 1813. It rose from the ashes to become a prosperous industrial centre, a summer holiday resort and finally a tourist attraction. It is also important for its architectural heritage with the largest number of pre-1850 buildings in the province. All these aspects are shown in the Museum's changing displays. To appreciate the town's role in the history of Canada, one must begin with a visit to the Niagara Historical Society Museum.

Niagara Historical Society Museum

Fireplace and "accessories" from the 1784-1810 period.

On the mantlepiece at the extreme right is an early toaster. The rack with slices of bread inserted was placed on the hearth close to the fire.

In the centre is a candle mold, next to a one-quart measure.

The notched implement hanging in the fireplace at the left is a trammel hook, used to adjust the height of the kettle over the fire. The notches were used to change the length of the hook.

Niagara Historical Society Museum

Bedroom, 1840-1850.

A four-poster bed made by Alexander Swinton, a Niagara carpenter, for his wife circa 1837. Its canopy rests on seven wooden bars which form an arch.

The chair has pine "thumb-back" supports with a triple-slat back, and a solid pine seat. Painted black with yellow and green floral stencilling on the seat and back circa 1825-1840, it shows a Germanic influence.

The shelf clock, circa 1840, is made by Sperry and Shaw, New York. Its construction is mahogany veneer on walnut.

Niagara Historical Society Museum

On the right is a judge's chair circa 1820-1830 used in both the 1817 Court House and the present Court House on Queen Street.

On the left, a tall case clock circa 1840. The case is made in Country Chippendale style by William Willox of Niagara-on-the-Lake, and the works are by William Donald of Scotland.

Niagara Historical Society Museum

Donated by Mrs. J.D. Servos, this military strongbox circa 1800-1820 has a hinged lid with handle and two carrying handles on the sides. Iron braces and straps form a pattern of squares with rounded knobs.

The Whale Inn, 66 King Street.

The Whale Inn sits at the foot of King Street on a piece of land boasting one of the best views in Ontario.

Built circa 1835 on property leased from the Niagara Harbour and Dock Company, the inn catered to sailors and merchants at the Dock. The tap room door at the left front of the house still bears witness to the building's early function.

For over 100 years the Elliott family owned the property. Innkeeper Walter, the first occupant, was succeeded by his son Thomas, a fisherman whose wife and then daughters operated a boarding house in the building. After the death of Adelaide, the last of the Elliott daughters, it became a private residence.

In the 1950's Mr. and Mrs. Oppenheimer and master carpenter Carl Banke restored the inn, and from 1972 to 1989 it was lovingly cared for by the late Mr. and Mrs. John Gwynne.

The Niagara-on-the-Lake Fire Museum.

The Niagara-on-the-Lake Fire Museum is located at the old Fire Station on King Street near the intersection of Queen. On display is fire fighting equipment preserved over the years by the members of the Volunteer Fire Department of Niagara-on-the-Lake. This collection allows the viewer to imagine how fires were fought in the early days and to see the advancements made in the field, from the primitive leather bucket to the sophisticated 1930's fire truck with its power driven pump. A leather bucket along with axe and long-handled hook were part of a fireman's equipment since the establishment of the first fire brigades. Although the leather bucket has long since become outmoded, the axe and hook are still in use today.

On display in the museum are a number of early portable hand pumps, an early professionally made hand-drawn water cart, a hand-drawn ladder wagon, and a hand-drawn hose cart. The museum is operated by the Niagara Historical Society.

The Moore House, 244 King Street.

This building on Crooks' New Survey land was probably erected as a four-bay structure with an off-centre doorway by Francis Moore, who bought the lot in 1828. From 1848 till the early 1890's it was owned by the Dorrity family, first Thomas, an innkeeper, and then John, a painter. In 1892 Jack Bishop bought the house and he and then his two sons owned it for over 70 years, the two sons sharing the 13-room dwelling as a "duplex".

The Bishops had a grocery business, first on Queen Street and then, after 1913, in the building now the Luis House.

Restoration architect Dr. Peter Stokes and his wife who bought the house about 20 years ago have restored many of its original features, including the cornice gutters, with great care and sympathy.

Masonic Hall, King and Prideaux streets.

In order to have a permanent meeting place, the Masons in 1791 erected a two-storey wooden building, the upper floor to be used for Masonic meetings and the lower floor with a large hall to be available for various other purposes. Records show that the hall was used by the local Agricultural Society as well as for community social events.

Since Lieutenant Governor Simcoe was himself a Mason, it is presumed that the first Parliament of Upper Canada was held in the hall on September 17, 1792. During the War of 1812 the building was destroyed, forcing the Masons thereafter to meet at various locations around Niagara. Shortly after the war, in 1816, some of the destroyed and burned buildings were renovated or rebuilt, and on the ruins of the Lodge a large stone structure was constructed which was used at various times as a private school, a hotel and military barracks.

When the great fire of 1860 devastated the town, the Masons rented the stone building on King and Prideaux streets, where the original Lodge of 1791 had been located. Seventeen years later the Masons decided to purchase the building with the intention of restoring it. Today a sign on the wall states "Niagara Lodge, No. 2, A.F. & A.M.—1792".

The Prince of Wales, Picton and King streets.

In the 1860's, Long's Hotel greeted travellers at the corner of King and Picton streets in Niagara-on-the-Lake. This rustic building was replaced by the Victorian style three-storey building of today measuring about 30 feet along Picton Street. From this period to the turn of the century, the hotel was known variously as the Arcade Hotel, Niagara House, Long's Hotel, and finally, The Prince of Wales Hotel.

After the Duke and Duchess of York (later King George V and Queen Mary) visited the town in 1901, the hotel was formally renamed "The Prince of Wales".

It passed through several hands before being purchased by Henry Wiens in 1975. Mr. Wiens began an extensive redecorating and expansion program, including property acquisitions along King Street, then Picton Street. Room accommodation and dining facilities were increased to meet the town's increasing popularity as a theatre centre and tourist attraction.

Burns House, 255 King Street

Though generally known as the Burns House, the building probably precedes Burns' ownership of the property. It is reputed to have been an inn and it was certainly owned by two Niagara licensees, Richard Howard in the 1830's and Mary Flinn in the late 1840's.

The Powell House, 433 King Street.

A letter to Mrs. Dummer Powell records that her son, John, had started to rebuild on the site of the earlier Powell house burned in 1813, and was living in two rooms and a kitchen in April, 1817. John Powell's family lived in the house until about 1836 when it was acquired by James Boulton, a barrister.

The Niagara myth that John Powell's sister-in-law, Sophia Shaw, was General Brock's fiancee has never been authenticated.

463 King Street.

    This fine brick building at the corner of King and Mary streets was for many years the home of T. Fred Best, long-time member of council, mayor from 1897 to 1901 and again in 1912, and owner of a prosperous butcher's shop on Queen Street. He bought the corner lot in 1885 from his father-in-law, Stephen Follet, and apparently built this house the same year. In recent years the building has been used as an art gallery.

The Wilderness, 407 King Street.

The four-acre Wilderness in the middle of town was given by the Six Nations Indians to the widow of Indian Agent Daniel Claus. Her original house, built on the bank of One Mile Creek which meanders through the property, was burned in December 1813.

Records show that the part of the present house to the right of the front door was occupied as early as 1816. By 1817 William Claus, his father's successor as Indian Agent, was building a matching addition to the left of the door and was also planting many varieties of trees on the land.

Over 170 years later, this fine, multi-treed estate remains one of the vital components of the town.

The Cameron House, 708 King Street.

This one-storey gable-roof house located at the south end of King Street in the area added to the town immediately after the War of 1812-14 was built for the well-to-do widow Cameron in 1817. Only four rooms in size, it is a small gem notable for its arcaded brick similar to that of the second Niagara Court House that was once its neighbour, for its two corner fireplaces and for lots of highly-decorative trim.

Together with the Court House, it became at one time part of Miss Rye's Western Home for Girls, and it has managed to survive its larger more imposing neighbour, but just barely.

Glen Smith has spent several years stabilizing and restoring the house, carefully researching each stage of the process. He still has "miles to go" but his efforts have already shown significant results.

The Pillar and Post, King and John streets.

What was once a successful canning factory for almost 40 years, processing local fruit and vegetables, has become today one of the most prestigious and luxurious hotels in the area for tourists and business people.

It is a very interesting place, which began on a small scale with a dining room, and provided accommodations for travellers. Now, the establishment offers a large swimming pool, a well-supplied handicraft shop, meeting rooms and numerous other facilities.

While in Niagara to attend the opening of the new Shaw Theatre in 1973, the Queen and Prince Philip made a stopover for dinner at the Pillar and Post.

175 Regent Street.

  Thomas Daly, a carpenter, bought this lot from lawyer James Boulton in 1848, built a house prior to 1850, and lived in it until 1883. Later, Robert Burns, a prominent Queen Street merchant, rented the house from Robert Bishop, another merchant.

The Eckersley House, 58 Johnson Street.

Usually referred to as the Eckersley House after the family who owned it from 1901 until the 1960's, the nucleus of this dwelling was built circa 1835 and its doorcase resembles that of one of its contemporaries, the Richardson-Kiely House on Queen Street. The original building was upgraded by Robert Fizette, a ship's carpenter and builder in the 1870's. He apparently left three souvenir $10 bills, two dated 1875 and one 1863, nailed to the wall frame behind the plaster. These were discovered during renovations in the 1960's.

Like the Vanderlip House (96 Johnson Street), this building had a porch that was removed in 1907 because it encroached on the sidewalk.

The Post House, 95 Johnson Street.

There is no question about the date of the original part of this house. It is carved on the keystone over the front door.

James Blain, a master mason and probably one of the contractors of St. Andrew's Church, built the house in 1835 and conducted a brick supply business from the rear yard. The building has also been used as a post office and as a private school. Early this century it was for many years the home of Sarah Lansing and it is still sometimes referred to as the "Lansing House".

The fine entrance with fanlight set in a moulded surround supported by fluted pillars enriches the simple, perfectly symmetrical facade of the early building. The section at the right was added in 1985.

The Vanderlip House, circa 1816, 96 Johnson Street.

Sometimes called the "Painter House" after the Painter-Gilmour family that occupied the building for about 100 years beginning in 1840, the house was once thought, incorrectly, to have survived the fire of December 1813. The upper windows at the front were added in the 1960's.

The George Varey House, circa 1835, 105 Johnson Street.

The two-storey building with Regency style roughcast finish and low pitched hipped roof was built on the fire-damaged foundation of a pre-1812 house by George Varey, a tailor and player of the bass viol at the Methodist church.

The *Times* newspaper of September 8, 1899 recorded that this fine house, plus three "tenements" nearby on Johnson Street also owned by Varey, had been sold for $1500.

118 Johnson Street.

Probably built circa 1835 by Jared Stocking, owner of a lucrative hat business in Niagara, the building became an inn known as the Sign of the Crown when it was sold to William Moffat in 1836. Apparently not a success as a tavern, it was used as an evening school in the late 1830's and as a boarding school (the York Academy) in the 1870's. More recently it was the home of W.E. Lyall, town clerk of Niagara, and his daughter Jessie.

Originally this building sat close to the street line.

126 Johnson Street.

This relatively early house circa 1828, probably another of George Varley's houses, is remembered in Niagara as the home of the Platt family, builders of fine carriages. Next to it stood several carriage shop buildings which were torn down and replaced by the house at No. 134 in the late 20's or early 30's.

Greenlees House, 135 Johnson Street.

George Greenlees, Yeoman, who bought a small lot with 41 feet frontage on Johnson Street from John MacMonigle in 1821, built this house circa 1822. In 1829 he added the Gate Street corner of the lot. Four years later he sold the property to innkeeper Lewis Donally, for 200 pounds, a considerable sum in those days. Lawyer Charles L. Hall, a frequent buyer and seller of real estate (he kept a personal plan of the town with lot owners inked in), acquired the building in 1842 and rented it as did his daughters who inherited his estate. One of the lessees, Noble Keith, was, like Donally, an innkeeper.

144 Johnson Street.

Deborah Muirhead, wife of Dr. James Muirhead, sold this property to Ralph Clement in the 1840's. The sale price, 257 pounds, suggests that a house existed at that time. For many years Major Joseph Clement occupied the house. After his death the building was extensively renovated by Andy Melbourne, a Niagara Falls businessman.

The Davidson House, circa 1845, 164 Johnson Street.

Built by Alex Davidson on land bought from the trustees of Robert Pilkington, a favourite aide of Mrs. Simcoe, the house was owned for most of this century by Alfred Ball and his daughter Kathleen, both prominent members of the Niagara Historical Society.

The original portion of the house displays many Greek Revival features typical of the 1840's. The newer side and rear wings are sympathetic additions designed by St. Catharines architect Jack McCallum.

The Clench House, 234 Johnson Street.

The main five-bay section of the house facing the garden was built between 1816 and 1824 by Ralph Clench, a former officer in Butler's Rangers who became Niagara's first town clerk and a member of the provincial parliament. It replaced a house that had miraculously escaped the great fire of December 1813 only to be destroyed accidentally a short time later by sparks from a wash day fire.

The Clench family owned the house until 1889 when J. Geale Dickson bought it and did some renovations.

The exteriors to the side and rear appear to have been added by Marie V. Holmwood, owner in the 1920's, and the front porch was added by Charles Hahn who bought the estate in the late 1940's.

The Lyons House, 8 Centre Street.

Catherine Geale (nee Claus) acquired the one-acre lot from her mother in 1833 and shortly thereafter she also acquired a husband, lawyer and county registrar John Lyons.

The Regency-style house, built circa 1835, passed from Catherine Geale Lyons to John B. Geale in 1867 and it remained Geale property till close to the end of the 19th century.

The house is one of the exceptions to the "rule" that early houses in town were built close to the street line. Its roughcast-over-brick finish is typical Regency, as is the use of deceits or blind windows to balance the design of the facade. (There is a fireplace, not a window, behind one set of "shutters"). The side wing is an addition probably made by J.B. Geale.

Breakenridge-Ure House, 240 Centre Street.

John Breakenridge, a barrister who came to Niagara from Virginia shortly after the War of 1812-14, built this two-storey brick house circa 1823 after having built 363 Simcoe Street and 392 Mississauga Street on the same four-acre block. Following his untimely death at the age of 39 in 1828, his widow, needing cash, held a school in the building. At present the house is in need of restoration.

St. Andrew's Presbyterian Church, Simcoe Street.

The cornerstone of this church, which replaced a 1796 church which burned in 1813, was laid on May 31, 1831. St. Andrew's is noted for its fine Greek Revival portico, box pews and exquisitely detailed pulpit, built in 1840 of native black walnut by master carpenter John Davidson. The building was restored in 1937.

St. Andrew's Church manse, corner of Simcoe and Centre Streets.

The manse was built in 1836 by Dr. Robert McGill, who had a few years earlier "organized" the building of the 1831 church across the street.

McGill, fifth minister of St. Andrew's, served the church from 1829-1845, giving the congregation stability over the years.

The congregation purchased the manse from Dr. McGill, apparently with money left as a legacy by Rev. John Young, St. Andrew's second minister (1802-1805).

The Butler House, 275 Simcoe Street.

The house was moved to its present site from original Butler lands at the southern edge of town on Mississauga Street, just beyond Ann Street.

Its origins are somewhat vague. Some believe it is part of Col. John Butler's house, others that it was built by his brother James, and others that it belonged to a descendant, Magistrate Johnson Butler. In the middle of the 19th century it was owned by James Butler, a farmer, and later by the Bissell family, one of whose members, now in her nineties, recalls a large wing at the rear of the building.

Dr. Peter Stokes, who was engaged to restore the building dates it circa 1815.

"Storrington" 289 Simcoe Street.

The one-acre lot on which this house stands was sold to Niagara innkeeper Charles Koune by Christopher Van Sicklin in 1810. In 1837 Koune resold the property to Jane Stocking and she in turn leased it "for life" to the Kounes.

Though the Lincoln County registry abstract of the lot makes no mention of James Lockhart, the man traditionally credited with building the house circa 1817, an advertisement in April 1837 that offered "for rent a two storey brick dwelling house with out-houses, garden and orchard...lately occupied by James Lockhart" establishes a connection.

The 1837 deed of sale to Jane Stocking also mentions Lockhart's occupancy of the house but not his ownership. Perhaps Lockhart leased the house before buying the Richardson House (209 Queen Street) in 1836, and Koune may have been the builder.

This is a typical Niagara house with end chimneys and a well-balanced facade. The original brick has been covered with stucco smoothed and jointed to look like stone.

The Creen House, 363 Simcoe Street.

The original house on this site was believed to be the first of three built on the four-acre block by lawyer John Breakenridge (see Breakenridge-Hawley and Breakenridge-Ure houses on Mississauga Street) who bought this one-acre lot in 1816 and sold it in three pieces by 1820. The last piece was bought by Alexander Garrett who resold to John Ross for 200 pounds in 1824. Four years later Ross sold to Thomas Creen, second rector of St. Mark's Church, for 203 pounds, 15 shillings and 6 pence. Creen's wife and two daughters inherited the building in 1861.

The original house was a one-and-a-half storey gabled building 36 feet by 18 feet. This was extended to the left and to the rear to create a salt box, perhaps by the Reverend, a classics scholar who took private pupils, some of them apparently boarders (he declared a household of 9 in 1848).

387 Simcoe Street.

This modern house, a Williamsburg reproduction built for dentist Dr. Clark and set well back from the sidewalk, is an attractive part of the Simcoe Street streetscape.

408 Simcoe Street.

The house at the southeast corner of Simcoe and William streets was built in 1904 by John Elliott, a fine mason as was his son Jim. The Elliotts built the pool and the wall at the Randwood Estate on John Street.

Breakenridge-Hawley House, 392 Mississauga Street.

The house at the corner of William and Mississauga streets is the second and today the most magnificent of three houses built on this four-acre block by Virginia lawyer, John Breakenridge.

Breakenridge built this "elegant and tasty home" circa 1816 on the town lot originally deeded to Aaron (or Arent) Brant, one of the town's first elected officials.

After Breakenridge sold the house in 1823, it was owned at one time by the socially and politically prominent Dickson Family.

By the middle of this century, the building had deteriorated badly. The house was rescued, preserved and restored by Frank Hawley.

134 Victoria Street.

Recently restored, this storey-and-a-quarter frame cottage is one of those smaller dwellings that have contributed to the attractiveness of the town's older residential section. Samuel Winterbottom, who probably built the house circa 1835, left the house to his son William Bowers Winterbottom, a lawyer for 65 years and the oldest bencher in Ontario when he died in 1895.

Wilson-Kent House, 175 Victoria Street.

In 1816 merchant James B. Jones sold this lot to John Wilson, also a merchant. Wilson built this one-and-a-half storey clapboard frame house close to the street line, and apparently lived in it until his death circa 1852.

279 Victoria Street

This attractive clapboard dwelling was built for Simon Walsh, a blacksmith, probably in the 1830's, Walsh bought the one-acre at the corner of Victoria and Gage streets from Edward Vanderlip in 1819. His will indicated that he lived here prior to 1853. His widow deeded the quarter-acre piece on which this house stands to her daughter-in-law Catherine for five shillings and "love and natural affection" in 1874.

285 Victoria Street.

This modern house built in the 1980's replaced the much smaller home of Brian Doherty, founder of the Shaw Festival.

315 Victoria Street.

   This is a much-altered version of a simple one-and-a-half-storey frame house built circa 1850 for Henry Carlisle, a tailor. Until recently, this house incorporated the front porch from the Vanderlip House (see 96 Johnson Street).

The Miller House, 46 Mary Street.

An old letter provides evidence that the house was under construction in 1816 and that Wm. Duff Miller and his family expected to occupy it the following year. Miller, an officer in the Lincoln Militia and a pillar of St. Andrew's Church, ran a stationery store on Queen Street and also served as Inspector and Deputy Clerk of the Crown and Pleas. His new house was thus conveniently located halfway between his two places of business. He and his wife Ann (nee Vansickle) had seven sons and five daughters and so this house must have originally accommodated fourteen people. Mrs. Miller is said to have planted many willows, brought from the Wilderness, on the grounds in 1816.

The Miller family owned the property until 1870; the following year it was acquired by the Hewgills who retained it until early this century.

The five-bay storey-and-a-half dwelling with large end chimneys retains its original charm and simplicity.

Dickson-Potter House, 94 John Street.

This Victorian cottage was built circa 1860 on a piece of land known as "the 23 acre field". The field itself can boast an illustrious list of owners. The names of Lt. Robert Pilkington (a favourite aide of Mrs. Simcoe), Chief Justice Elmsley, Hon. William Dickson and his son, Hon. Walter H., all appear on the registry office abstract.

This is a typical, rather picturesque Victorian cottage in an especially delightful setting.

Brunswick Place or Pinehurst, John Street.

The house is situated on John Street next to Randwood. The oldest part was built circa 1830 by Captain Melville, Manager of the Niagara Harbour and Dock Co., who bought the land from the Hon. William Dickson family. Towards the end of the 19th century it was bought by Captain Robert G. Dickson, grandson of Hon. William. Captain Dickson introduced golf to Niagara-on-the-lake.

Later owners were the H.P. Bissell family and the Letchworth family, American summer residents. The present owner is artist, Tricia Romance.

The Shaw Theatre.

The Shaw Festival. Photo D. Cooper

The Shaw Theatre, The Commons.

The Shaw Festival began in 1962 when a small group of theatre enthusiasts comprised of Brian Doherty, Calvin Rand, Jean Marsh, John Couillard and Jim and Marie Usher met at a private dinner party. They felt that a summer theatre would be ideal for Niagara-on-the-Lake.

At the first public meeting which attracted about 40 interested people, it was decided to feature George Bernard Shaw and promote the project as "A Salute to Shaw", choosing "Candida" and "Don Juan in Hell" as the first plays.

In the hot summer of 1962 the historic Court House on Queen Street was converted into a small theatre. On the steps of the magnificent building stood two young ushers holding a banner with the words "Salute to Shaw". The theatre doors were open for eight weeks and ten unpaid actors and helpers under the direction of Maynard Burgess made an amazing impact on the attending public. As a reward for their efforts, in 1965 the Festival received its first grant of $10,000 from the Ontario Arts Council.

The Shaw Festival proved a great success and by the end of the 1960's it became evident that the Festival was in desperate need of a new and larger permanent facility to continue its work. Toronto architect Ron Thom was chosen to design a new theatre to be located on what is known as the Commons, not far from Wellington Street.

On April 17, 1972, Brian Doherty, founder of the Shaw Festival, turned the first sod for a modern theatre designed to blend architecturally into the historic atmosphere of Niagara-on-the-Lake. The theatre opened in 1973 with a 847-seat capacity. On June 28 of that year, Her Majesty Queen Elizabeth II and His Royal Highness the Duke of Edinburgh attended the performance of "You Never Can Tell".

392 Mississauga Street

58 Johnson Street

209 Queen Street

St. Andrew's Manse

69 Prideaux Street

463 King Street

St. Vincent de Paul Church

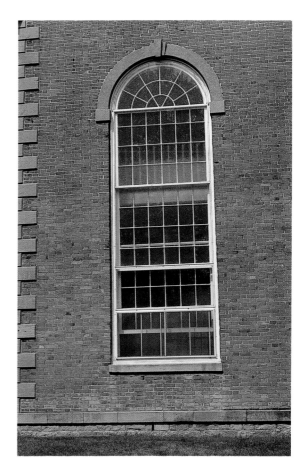

St. Andrew's Church

95 Johnson Street

Index

Acknowledgements, 4
Angel Inn, 30

Bank of Montreal, 36
Breakenridge-Hawley House, 105
Burberry Cottage, 46
Butler's Barracks, 19
Burns House, 79
Butler's Burying Ground, 20
Butler's Graveyard Plaques, 21
Butler House, 100

Cameron House, 83
Campbell House, 65
Centre Street #240, 97
Clench House, 95
Clock Tower, 25
Court House, 31
Creen House, 102

Daly-Alma Store, 33
Davidson House, 94
Dee Building, 34
Demeath, 54
Dickson-Potter House, 112
Dover House, 66

Eckersley House, 86

Fort George, 15, 16, 17, 18
Fort Mississauga, 24
Front Street #10, 59
Front Street #26, 58

Gazebo, 113
Greenlees House, 92

Hiscott House, 55
Historic Background, 5

Johnson Street #118, 90
Johnson Street #126, 91
Johnson Street #144, 93

King Street #463, 81
Kirby House, 56

Lyons House, 96

MacDougal House, 44
Malcolmson House, 67
Masonic Hall, 77
McClelland's West End Store, 38

Miller house, 111
Moffatt Inn, 64
Moore House, 76
Muirhead, Dr. James, 47

Navy Hall, 22
Niagara Apothecary, 26, 27, 28
Niagara Fire Hall Museum, 75
Niagara Historical Society, 69, 70, 71, 72, 73
Niagara location, 7

Oban Inn, The, 57

Parliament, First Opening of, 13, 14
Pillar and Post, 84
Post House, 87
Powell House, 80
Prideaux Street #31, 48
Prideaux Street #59, 53
Prideaux Street #69, 54
Prince of Wales, 78
Promenade House, 52
Public School, Old, 68

Queen Street #118, 42
Queen Street #122-124, 40

Regent Street #175, 85
Richardson-Kiely House, 45
Rogers-Harrison House, 43
Rowley Block, 35
Royal George Theatre, 41

St. Andrew's Presbyterian Church, 98, 99
St. Mark's Church, 61, 62, 63
St. Vincent de Paul Church, 60
Shaw Theatre, 114, 115
Sherlock Block, 32
Sign of the Pineapple, 29
Simcoe Monument, 23
Simcoe Street #387, 103
Simcoe Street #408, 104
Squire Clements, 37
Stewart House, 49, 50, 51
"Storrington", 101

Vanderlip House, 88
Varey House, 89
Victoria Street #134, 106
Victoria Street #279, 108
Victoria Street #285, 109
Victoria Street #315, 110

Whale Inn, 74
Wilderness, 82
Wilson-Kent House, 107